D1716633

THE BULLY-FREE ZONE

WHEN PEOPLE BULLY WITH WORDS

THERESE HARASYMIW

PowerKiDS
press.
New York

Published in 2021 by The Rosen Publishing Group, Inc.
29 East 21st Street, New York, NY 10010

First Edition

Portions of this work were originally authored by Addy Ferguson and published as *Bullying with Words: Teasing, Name-Calling, and Rumors*. All new material in this edition authored by Therese Harasymiw.

Editor: Therese M. Shea
Book Design: Reann Nye

Photo Credits: Cover Pixel-Shot/Shutterstock.com; series art Here/Shutterstock.com; p. 5 Phil Boorman/ Cultura/Getty Images; p. 7 Tassii/E+/Getty Images; p. 8 FatCamera/E+/Getty Images; p. 9 Diego Cervo/Shutterstock.com; p. 11 Akiko Aoki/ Moment/Getty Images; p. 13 Lopolo/Shutterstock.com; p. 14 PeopleImages/E+/Getty Images; pp. 15, 21 SDI Productions/E+/Getty Images; p. 17 kali9/E+/ Getty Images; p. 19 © iStockphoto.com/hanapon1002; p. 20 kate_sept2004/E+/Getty Images; p. 22 Fertnig/E+/Getty Images.

Library of Congress Cataloging-in-Publication Data

Names: Harasymiw, Therese, author.
Title: When people bully with words / Therese Harasymiw.
Description: New York : PowerKids Press, [2021] | Series: The bully-free
    zone | Includes index.
Identifiers: LCCN 2019057365 | ISBN 9781725319448 (paperback) | ISBN
    9781725319462 (library binding) | ISBN 9781725319455 (6 pack)
Subjects: LCSH: Bullying—Juvenile literature. | Invective—Juvenile
    literature. | Verbal self-defense—Juvenile literature.
Classification: LCC BF637.B85 H3554 2021 | DDC 302.34/3—dc23
LC record available at https://lccn.loc.gov/2019057365

Manufactured in the United States of America

Some of the images in this book illustrate individuals who are models. The depictions do not imply actual situations or events.

CPSIA Compliance Information: Batch #CSPK20. For Further Information contact Rosen Publishing, New York, New York at 1-800-237-9932.

Find us on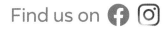

CONTENTS

DIFFERENT KINDS OF BULLIES

Bullies hurt others. They pick on those they think are weaker or different. They hurt, scare, **embarrass**, or leave them out.

Physical bullies use their bodies to bully. They push, hit, or harm their victim. Social bullies get people to **ignore** or leave others out of activities. They may lie or spread stories about someone. Cyberbullies use the internet. They write texts, emails, and online posts to hurt people. Verbal bullies use words to **threaten** or hurt others. This book is about verbal bullies and what you can do to stop them from hurting you and others with their words.

Sometimes, people aren't just one kind of bully. They might be verbal and physical bullies, for example.

5

IS IT VERBAL BULLYING?

You might wonder what the difference is between bullying with words and joking. Friends tease each other at times. Both friends take part. They speak their words in fun. The teasing stops if one asks for it to stop. It should stop if someone becomes uncomfortable too.

The words of verbal bullies aren't about fun. They're used to harm. They may be used to make the bully feel more powerful. Verbal bullies keep bullying even if someone says to stop. In fact, the **taunting**, name-calling, and other hurtful words may get worse once the bully knows their victim is upset.

IN THE ZONE

Verbal bullies may use words that hurt about weight, appearance, or the way someone acts.

EXAMPLES OF VERBAL BULLYING:

- Teasing
- Name-calling
- Taunting
- Threatening harm

People who bully with words may write them too.

WORDS HURT

From the outside, verbal bullying may seem like it's no big deal. You might think a person should be able to ignore hurtful words. It's not that easy, though.

IN THE ZONE

Bullied kids are more likely to miss school, which can hurt their grades.

Victims of bullying may have trouble sleeping and eating.

Verbal bullying can have serious and lasting effects. Imagine being afraid to go to school for fear that a bully will tease you in front of everyone. The victim can feel **depressed**, angry, embarrassed, and scared—even if they try not to show it. The victims of bullies often withdraw from activities. They end up feeling lonely. Even after the bullying stops, these feelings may not go away.

WHO IS A TARGET?

People who bully feel more powerful than their victim in some way. Bullies often pick on certain people believing no one will stand up for them. They may look for victims who don't fit in. These people may look or act different in some way. They may have different interests too. Those with **disabilities**, those who are shy, and those who seem to have few friends are common victims.

The bully may focus their hurtful words on these or other features. We're all different in some way, so we all could be bullied. It's never the victim's fault.

Bullying can happen anywhere,
inside and outside of school.

WHY BULLIES BULLY

Why would someone want to hurt another person with words? Most bullies like the feeling of power because they feel powerless sometimes. Bullying may make them feel better about something bad happening in their lives. Bullies may learn this way of acting from parents, older brothers or sisters, or other people in their home. Some bullies are bullied by others in their lives. Bullies also might want attention or are trying to make others feel like they do. They may have low **self-esteem** too.

None of these is a good reason for hurting other people. Bullying is wrong, no matter what's behind it.

Some bullies are just acting like their friends, who are also bullies. It's still wrong.

13

HOW TO REACT

You might think that the best way to stop a verbal bully is to fight. It's not. Fighting could get you hurt. It also may make you look like the bully and get you into trouble!

IN THE ZONE

Bullies are much more likely to stop bullying if someone stands up for the bullied person.

Sometimes saying that a way of acting is bullying is a good way to make a bully back off.

There are several ways to **react** to a bully. The one to choose may depend on how you feel at the moment and how the bully might react. You could try ignoring the bully. No reaction may make them stop. You could be forceful and tell them to leave you alone. If either of these actions doesn't stop the bullying, you'll have to get help.

SEEKING HELP

If bullying continues after the bully is told to stop, it's important to tell someone. Kids who are being bullied may think that telling someone will not help or that it might make the bullying worse. However, that's not true. Bullying can be dangerous. Adults should be ready to act.

If the bullying is happening at school, a trusted teacher can stop it before it happens again to you or someone else. A parent or school **counselor** can help kids who are bullied deal with their feelings. An adult in your corner will make you feel stronger too.

Talking about how you're feeling after being bullied will make you feel better.

UNDOING THE DAMAGE

Verbal bullying can affect your self-esteem. However, there are ways to fight back and feel good about yourself again. Remember the bully doesn't know you well. You know yourself, and your friends and family know you. As mean as a bully's words might be, they don't change the person you are.

If you're feeling lonely or depressed, talk to a parent, friend, or counselor. These people can help you see the good things that they like about you. They can help you realize that being bullied isn't your fault. Talking to someone about it is an important step to feeling better.

IN THE ZONE

It's important for someone who has been bullied to make connections with other people. Staying home and away from friends can be harmful.

Setting a goal and working toward it is a good way to fight the bad feelings that come from being bullied.

19

SCHOOLS VS. BULLIES

Many schools have been successful in fighting the bullying problem. Principals, teachers, and students can work together to create bully-free zones. They find ways to teach students to have **compassion** and respect for each other. They use anti-bullying messages in many classes. They work toward creating a positive school **environment** for all.

Studies have shown that anti-bullying programs in school can make a difference in fighting a bullying problem.

Talk to a principal or teacher about starting a program to rid your school of bullying if it doesn't have one. If your school's anti-bullying program isn't working, you should talk to someone about changing it. Keep in mind that a bully-free zone takes time.

BE AN ANTI-BULLYING HERO

Standing up for yourself against a bully isn't easy. Neither is standing up for your friends. Taking on a bully requires bravery and brains. Sometimes, seeking help from an adult is the brave *and* smart thing to do to fight bullying.

Standing up for people you don't know or don't like is even harder. However, it's still the right thing to do. If you were being bullied, wouldn't you want someone on your side? Everyone deserves to be treated with respect and compassion. If bullies realized that, they wouldn't be bullies. You might be the hero that someone needs today.

GLOSSARY

compassion: A feeling of wanting to help someone who is hurt or in trouble.

counselor: Someone who talks with people about their feelings and who gives advice.

depressed: Feeling sad, hopeless, or unimportant.

disability: A problem that makes it difficult for a person to do certain things.

embarrass: To cause somebody to be ashamed or ill at ease.

environment: Everything that surrounds someone and affects the way they live.

ignore: To do nothing about or in response to something. Also, to pretend not to notice.

react: To behave or change in a particular way when something happens.

self-esteem: A feeling of having respect for yourself.

taunt: To insult someone to make them angry or hurt.

threaten: To say that you will harm someone, often to get something.

INDEX

WEBSITES

Due to the changing nature of Internet links, PowerKids Press has developed an online list of websites related to the subject of this book. This site is updated regularly. Please use this link to access the list: www.powerkidslinks.com/bullyfree/words